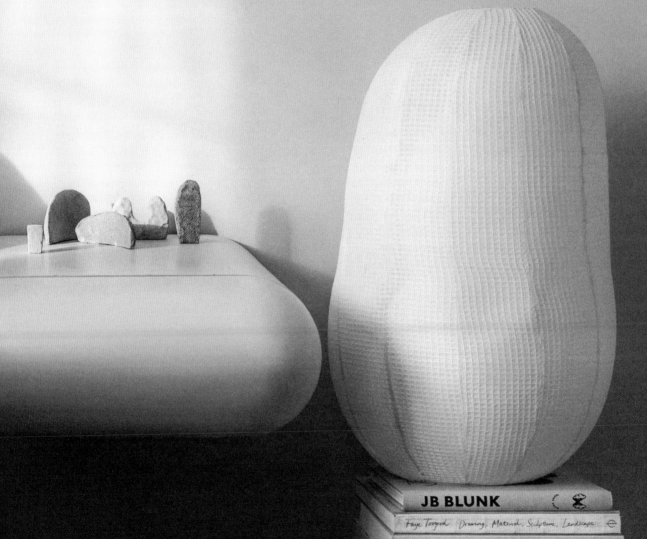

JB BLUNK

Faye Toogood   Drawing, Material, Sculpture, Landscape

STONE

THE TOUCH

creative homes

creative homes

EVOCATIVE, ECLECTIC &
CAREFULLY CURATED HOMES

ANNA MALMBERG / MARI STRENGHIELM

RYLAND PETERS & SMALL
LONDON • NEW YORK

Designer Paul Tilby

Senior Commissioning Editor
  Annabel Morgan
Editor Sophie Devlin
Creative Director Leslie Harrington
Head of Production Patricia Harrington

First published in 2024 by
Ryland Peters & Small
20–21 Jockey's Fields
London WC1R 4BW
and
341 E 116th Street
New York, NY 10029
www.rylandpeters.com

Text copyright © Mari Strenghielm 2024
Photography copyright © Anna
Malmberg 2024
Design copyright © Ryland Peters
& Small 2024

The author's moral rights have been
asserted. All rights reserved. No part of this
publication may be reproduced, stored in a
retrieval system, or transmitted in any form
or by any means, electronic, mechanical,
photocopying, recording, or otherwise,
without prior consent of the publisher.

British Library Cataloguing-in-Publication
Data. A catalogue record for this book is
available from the British Library.

10 9 8 7 6 5 4 3 2 1

ISBN: 978-1-78879-593-7

Printed and bound in China

MIX
Paper | Supporting
responsible forestry
FSC® C008047

CONTENTS

INTRODUCTION

Anna and I first met in 2016. Working in the same field as an interior stylist and photographer, we shared a very similar aesthetic and were surely destined to meet sooner or later. Just a couple of months later, we collaborated for the very first time and have been working as a team ever since. The projects we have taken on together have been a great adventure, and in the process, we've become the best of friends.

The idea of a book on creative homes first occurred to us a few years back. It seemed a natural progression, as we visit so many interesting, inventive and artistic homes as we crisscross Europe shooting interiors for magazines and commercial clients. We are privileged to spend time in many stunning locations while on photo shoots. However, visiting the talented and varied creatives included in this book in their own homes has been a truly inspiring and meaningful experience for us both. Each home reflects the particular creative endeavours and preoccupations of its inhabitants and gives us an insight into their very different processes, inspirations and ways of life.

The artists, sculptors, designers, textile artists, ceramicists and others featured here generously welcomed us with open arms, and it has been an honour to document their homes and work. We hope our selection of creative homes will inspire readers to look at their own homes with different eyes and to feel a sense of freedom when it comes to decorating. We are all creative in our own way, and where can we give expression to that innate human impulse to make, to create and to beautify if not at home? There are so many ideas here to enjoy and emulate, whether you are a calm-loving minimalist or someone who revels in dramatic and colourful interiors. We hope you enjoy visiting these creative homes just as much as we did.

NATURALLY CREATIVE

Textile artist Adriana and ceramicist and painter Jaume met when Jaume was living close to the rocky bay of Cala s'Almunia on the southeast coast of Mallorca and Adriana was based in the next village. The pair would bump into each other when walking on the beach, but nothing more than friendly chatting happened at that time. It wasn't until about 10 years later that the two met again and fell in love.

Adriana's passion for textiles began when she moved to Barcelona to study fashion design. She discovered that the fashion world was not the right fit for her, but her studies sparked a fascination with textiles that has led to the evolution of her unique artworks. The couple's first home together was a house in the small town of Ses Salines in southern Mallorca, and it was while living here that Adriana developed an interest in working with wool. Their closest neighbour was a shepherd and he and Adriana struck a deal: his flock could graze in Adriana and Jaume's garden, and in return he would pay her in shorn fleeces.

Jaume's mother had a ceramics studio in Palma and he grew up assisting her and his brother in the studio. But rather than following a traditional path, he yearned to do something different and began working in a more expressive way. The result is his delicate organic vessels and sculptural orb-shaped forms that draw inspiration from the natural world.

When Jaume started painting a series of huge canvases alongside his ceramics and Adriana needed more storage for her materials, the couple realized they had outgrown their space. After much searching, they found a new home through a friend who owns a design company called 2Monos producing handmade furniture. Adriana no longer has enough space to keep many sheep, but she still helps the shepherd with shearing and is paid in fleeces. She washes the wool and then uses it raw, incorporating it with native grasses and dried foliage and drawing upon traditional craft techniques. The resulting textile artworks are one of a kind and Adriana is starting to develop an international reputation.

Now happily ensconced on their farm in rural Campos, Adriana and Jaume have space to live and create as well as a large barn that functions as a showroom for their work. Converting this barn was no mean feat. The space had previously been used to store hay bales, so

Jaume and Adriana outside the entrance to their farmhouse near Campos, Mallorca with their sheepdog Tota (above left). Since moving here, the couple has carried out a gentle renovation of the dairy farm. They now both have their own workshops as well as a shared gallery space in the old barn (above right) where they display an ever-changing array of work. The ceramic pieces are by Jaume, while the raw wool is one of the fleeces Adriana uses in her artworks.

Jaume started by clearing it. Pigeons had roosted there for many years, so once the space had been emptied it required a second deep clean before the couple could transform it into the showroom space it is today.

Inside the house, the walls were painted white and a concrete floor was laid. The minimal, almost spartan surroundings reflect the way in which Adriana and Jaume like to live, surrounded only by essential pieces of furniture and a few treasured decorative pieces. They find that the stripped-back simplicity of the living spaces, with their rustic finishes and natural materials, helps to inspire the creative process. However, the space is in a constant state of flux, as the couple likes to live alongside recent pieces for a while before replacing them with newer work.

Besides their passion for creativity and handcrafts, Adriana and Jaume share a love for animals and their menagerie is growing fast. So far, its members are a goat called Petit, two sheep named Joana and Morritos, four chickens, two ducks and a flock of ducklings and two peacocks, plus cats Federico and Moyo and dog Tota.

The house is a typical Mallorcan finca, or farmhouse, with a terracotta plastered façade (below). Adriana and Jaume love animals and they keep adding family members to the farm. Seen here are Petit the goat and Federico the cat.

The couple spent a lot of time clearing out the upstairs of the barn, which they now use as a gallery and working space. In between the workshop and the gallery, Adriana and Jaume have created this small lounge area where they can entertain visiting clients and friends. The striking mid-century chairs are from a flea market in France and the painting on the wall was created to match by Jaume himself.

This central space leads to four out of five rooms in the house (opposite, clockwise from above left); Jaume's ceramicist brother Joan Pere Català made the plates on the kitchen sink; figurines handmade by Jaume on the kitchen shelf; a sculptural ocarina (traditional wind instrument) that was made in Mallorca. The couple decided to keep the old farmhouse kitchen just as it was when they arrived here (below).

Adriana's workshop actually consists of two rooms: in one she does all her weaving and in the other her sewing (above). Both spaces are painted white so that they feel light and fresh, allowing her creativity to flow. Federico the cat sits on the table in front of a textile art piece created by Adriana (opposite, clockwise from above left); a view into the serene bedroom; the beauty of natural light; a small gathering of ceramic pieces by Jaume on the floor of his workshop.

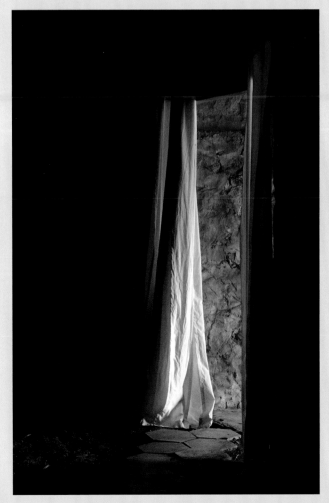

Adriana's studio has a homemade desk with legs built from wooden branches. The art piece is one of her latest designs made with linen and straw. A selection of the natural materials she uses in her work can be seen throughout the room in a neat and tidy display.

This is the combined living and dining room (above and opposite). Before the couple moved into the house, they put a layer of concrete on all the floors and painted the walls white. They didn't need to do much more inside, as all the original features had been well preserved: the ceiling vaults, the wooden doors and windows and the roof beams.

Jaume's workshop occupies the ground floor of the barn, where the former owners once kept their cows. The space receives plenty of light and mess is not a concern. In a corner is an old Thonet rocking chair where Jaume sits when he needs a break (above). In front of the windows, he has built shelves where his ceramic pieces can dry out in the sunlight (opposite).

A full view of Jaume's studio with the pottery wheel in the middle facing the windows. On the right-hand side of the room, the foundations of the cattle's water and food bowls are still in place. Seen alongside Jaume's work, they have become a sculptural feature in their own right.

The old well in the yard is still frequently used, but mainly for the animals (opposite). In Mallorca you can buy peacocks at local markets. Fascinated by these beautiful creatures, the couple bought two for the farm, where they are free to roam but choose to stay (above). Their bright plumage stands out against the stone walls of the house.

AIM FOR THE MOON

One of the oldest buildings in central Paris is home to health guru and businesswoman Emma Sawko. In the space of the past decade, Emma has built a reputation as a global tastemaker working in Paris, New York and Dubai. She is also the mother of three young adult children.

Emma was born in New York to Parisian parents and studied hotel and restaurant management in Switzerland. A 12-year career in advertising in Paris followed, before she relocated with her husband and young family to New York, then Dubai. It was while living in Dubai that Emma founded Comptoir 102, a concept design store with a organic juice bar and cafe all under the same roof. It enjoyed huge success, leading Emma to open Wild & The Moon, a chain of plant-based, healthy eating restaurants that now has branches in Paris, Amsterdam and Dubai and is growing fast. Emma is also the author of *Wild Recipes*, a cookbook filled with the many healthy and delicious dishes she has created for the restaurants.

The flat where Emma lives is situated in the busy second arrondissement, right in the city centre. Despite this, it overlooks a sleepy street, a feature that's rare in this area. As Emma leads a busy life, home is somewhere she retreats to recharge her batteries, and the tranquil apartment feels far removed from the busy city outside.

Emma loves its charming architecture – the crooked staircase, sturdy beams and uneven terracotta floor tiles create something of a rustic mood. The space is organized around a large, light living room and the open-plan kitchen, where Emma spends time experimenting with new recipes for Wild & The Moon. 'My interior at home is a mix and match of things I love,' she explains. 'Through the years I've collected furniture and things from places I've lived, and a lot of things are mementoes that I've picked up during my travels.'

The apartment showcases intriguing vintage finds, lots of art and books and other quirky treasures, all set alongside design classics – Emma says she gravitates towards timeless pieces rather than trend-led looks. She enjoys reinventing her home, moving pieces around to refresh the interiors and breathe new life into the space.

'Since I was a little girl, I've been interested in places and what they have to offer,' Emma recounts. 'I think that travelling has enriched me, and if I'd have to pinpoint my interior style, I would say it's in between the American culture, as in cool and relaxed, and the French culture, chic and refined. These are my two nationalities.'

Over the years, Emma has created creative and deeply personal homes that are true to her own style, but her talent for interior design has now found a further outlet in the Wild & The Moon restaurants. She freely admits that she knows exactly how she wants everything to look, feel and taste when it comes to food, interiors and fashion. 'These topics inspire me in the same way as art does, and luckily enough I'm fortunate to work with developing these interests in my profession.' Having said that, 'Working with my passion isn't all hunky-dory,' Emma confesses. 'I am a workaholic and I have learned the hard way to force myself to stop and recharge.' As a result, she is disciplined about carving out the time for a workout every morning, and every now and again heads off to a yoga retreat for a complete mind and body reset.

It's said that you can learn a lot about someone by taking a peek at their bookshelves (above). Emma has a passion for reading and a curious mind. Here we find cookbooks, volumes about health and wellbeing and of course the odd decorative piece. Emma loves ceramics and is a keen collector of beautiful arts and crafts that make her happy. She enjoys creating still lifes from odd pieces with different shapes or forms and colours that harmonize together (left).

It's easy to understand how Emma fell in love with the rustic beams and worn floor tiles in her Parisian apartment, to which she has brought a touch of warmth and femininity with select designer details (pages 34–35). The dining area is furnished with a vintage Tulip dining table and chairs by Eero Saarinen (above). Near the fireplace, a collection of paintings and drawings hangs above a pair of 3D-printed Chubby chairs made from recycled plastic by the Dutch designer Dirk van der Kooij (opposite).

As Emma loves to cook, it's important to her that the kitchen is in the centre of the home (above). From here she can socialize with dining guests in the dining and living areas while preparing meals. The India Mahdavi table lamp casts a warm glow.

The eye-catching original fireplace still works and is frequently used by Emma, especially during autumn and winter when it's cold outside (opposite). The candles are lit whenever she is home all year round just to create a cosy and inviting atmosphere.

The bedroom in the apartment has been painted in a soft yellow colour, which complements the assortment of bed linens in beige, ochre and black (left). The brown fibreglass Roly-Poly chair was created by British designer Faye Toogood.

Looking into the bedroom through the modern black window frames reveals a cool clash between old and new (above). The side table is a vintage find from the 1970s. On top of it stands a Pipistrello lamp designed by Gae Aulenti for Martinelli Luce in 1965 – its name is the Italian word for bat because its curved shade resembles the outstretched wings of the flying mammal.

Soraya's home is constantly changing, so she has built a shelf space for the decorative items she has collected over the years (below). She uses them whenever she gets that sudden urge to rearrange things around the house. After returning from the Milan Furniture Fair, she felt so inspired that she created this artwork on a cabinet in the living room in just a day (opposite). The Togo sofa was designed by Michel Ducaroy for Ligne Roset and the coffee table was made by Soraya herself.

DUE NORTH

In Umeå, in the northeast of Sweden, artist Soraya Forsberg lives with her husband Michael and their six children in a beautiful wooden farmhouse dating back to the early 19th century. The family moved here from Stockholm – having grown tired of the stresses of a big city, they were seeking peace and quiet, more space for the children and a home where Soraya could give free rein to her creativity.

The couple was very familiar with the beautiful old property when it came up for sale. It had long been something of a dream house for them, and even though the building was in bad shape, they jumped at the chance to own it. About 300 sq. m/3,230 sq. ft in size, it was previously divided into two, one part being a shop run by the owners, who lived in the other part. The space in between and the entire upper floor were unused, and opening up this space was a priority when Soraya and Michael began work on the house. 'The old farm shop was the starting point for our renovation journey, as we needed a functional bathroom and more bedrooms. The equation just didn't add up – one bedroom, two hallways and a kitchen for eight people,' says Soraya.

Very little had been done to the house since it was built, bar a minor kitchen renovation and the addition of a bathroom in the 1950s. When Soraya and her family moved in, the walls were covered with yellowing paint or peeling wallpaper. There was plastic flooring everywhere, which was ripped up to reveal the original wooden floors that Soraya and Michael were able to restore.

The upstairs consisted of a chilly, uninsulated attic that was uninhabitable, despite the fact that the structure was in surprisingly good condition for the age of the house. Converting this space was the next big project for Soraya and Michael, and they reconfigured it as bedrooms for the children and two open-plan spaces. These are home to a games and reading corner with plenty of storage space, a crafting corner and an area for socializing. 'Our house should be a home where the kids have places where they can hide away and be by themselves if they want to, just as much as I want it to have places where the kids can hang out with their friends at all times,' Soraya explains. While renovating this area the couple also decided to reposition the staircase, which was poky and inconveniently situated, and this now leads straight upstairs from the living room instead.

Soraya loves to experiment with the decor in her home and says she is constantly playing with colours and shapes, structures and materials. Many of the pieces in this home have either been recycled or designed by Soraya, and the children never know quite what they will find when they come through the door – she may have changed rooms around, explored new colour combinations or tried some other inventive and unexpected ideas.

Recently Soraya has begun working from a new studio close to home. After exhibiting a series of artworks made from recycled plywood and paper with an online gallery she was snowed under with commissions, but it proved impossible to work on them at home, surrounded by her children and the family dog. Her new studio also doubles as an overflow space for her collection of vintage furniture, allowing Soraya to swap pieces in and out of the house as the mood takes her. She is also busy working on her own furniture designs and a series of wooden sculptures. It's evident that this home is a perpetual source of inspiration and creativity.

In the centre of the big house we find the living room, which has a staircase leading to the top floor. The wall lamp, by Serge Mouille for Mobelaris, is a mid-century design classic. Soraya designed the folding shutters, the tall shelving unit and the sculptural pillar.

This view from the living room towards the hallway reveals a glimpse of the hammock that Soraya built into the floor upstairs (opposite). Soraya is currently collaborating with a carpenter to create a series of artworks in wood – she sketches the forms and he carves (above left). The whole house is more or less a piece of art, even the roof (below left). The old timber wall in the hallway has been left raw and uncovered to showcase the fascinating history of the house (above right).

This is part of the lounge space upstairs that Soraya and Michael designed
for their children (above and opposite). They built the window seats and
the cupboards with the lovely arched doors. At the Saarinen Tulip table,
the kids do their homework or have a snack after school. Soraya took the
big mirror and painted around the edges to create a dynamic effect.

With a family of eight people, installing a staircase and renovating the upper floor took priority (above and opposite). This whole space now belongs to the kids. In addition to the bedrooms, Soraya had so much fun designing this creative space, which is filled with colour and texture. The low profiles of the furniture allow for the sloping ceilings.

Soraya is a multidisciplinary artist and her work is placed here and there all over the house, including the hallway (opposite). This doorway leads into the master bedroom, one of the only rooms in the house that Soraya has kept just white and neutral.

It's a serene place where her creative brain can get some rest. The bathroom, too, is simply and inexpensively decorated, but certainly not boring (above). The painted wood panelling creates tiny ledges for useful and decorative objects.

TAKING SHAPE

London's Clissold Park has a sleepy small-town vibe and its location, just around the corner from Stoke Newington's charming and lively Church Street, was what originally drew Tom Lawson and Tom Collison to their post-war flat on the Hawksley Court Estate.

The living room is bathed in sunlight in the afternoons (opposite above). From here the couple has access to the balcony with space both for socializing and for growing the herbs they use for their cooking. The walls, ceiling and built-in furniture have all been painted with a custom shade of white throughout the apartment, including in the bedroom (opposite below). The soft hue establishes a warm and cosy atmosphere in the home.

Tom Lawson is head of product at Aman Interiors, while his partner Tom Collison is a studio assistant for sculptor Antony Gormley as well as working on his own projects. The couple met at an exhibition where Tom (Collison) was taking part in Brompton Design Week and instantly connected over a shared passion for design. 'We got on really well, found that many of our other interests aligned and here we are, three years later!'

After purchasing the flat at the beginning of 2021, the two Toms spent four months stripping the space back to its bare bones before embarking on a renovation. 'Although the flat was in good condition when we purchased it, we felt we could improve it by changing the layout,' they explain. The wall between the tiny kitchen and living room was taken down, freeing up enough space for a dining area. 'As we both enjoy cooking and hosting, this was very important for us,' says Tom Collison. To enhance the newfound sense of space, the couple replaced the existing flooring with reclaimed boards painted glossy white to reflect every ray of available light.

The flat is not large, so the Toms wanted to simplify the interior and started by removing the door frames and skirting boards/baseboards throughout. Using Farrow & Ball's Strong White as a base, they mixed their own colour for the walls, naming it 'Barrie White', after their block. The velvety tone softens the architectural details and creates a calm, minimalist mood. It also allowed the couple to focus on combining different materials and textures to bring interest to the space. 'We used raw terracotta tiles from the outside entrance into the hall and in the bathroom. The imperfections and warm tones added character and created unity,' Tom Collison explains.

In the bedroom, the couple spent many hours sanding years of varnish off the wooden floors. They gave the walls and ceiling a layer of limewash and built a fitted wardrobe/closet, adding a sense of warmth and comfort.

Decorative inspiration was drawn from the homes of artists and designers. 'One of the main points of reference is the fireplace, which was inspired by Georgia O'Keeffe's fireplace in New Mexico. We've also been strongly influenced by Diego Rivera and Frida Kahlo's studio, which Tom [Lawson] visited in Mexico. We fell in love with the ExCinere tiles by Formafantasma for Dzek, which [were a] massive influence on the colours we used in the kitchen. We created a custom-built sideboard/credenza using yellow Valchromat, inspired by the Imi Knoebel MDF installation Raum 19.'

Another source of inspiration was the Potter's House in Son Servera, Mallorca, formerly the home and studio of ceramicist Maria Antonia Carrio and now the setting for artists' residencies. It encouraged Tom Lawson to hand-build a variety of ceramic pieces for the apartment, including door handles, lampshades and various pots.

A few minutes' walk away, Tom Collison rents a large studio with lots of natural light. It's shared with two other creatives: one a painter who creates her own paint from natural materials, and the other a seller of art and design pieces with an environmental focus.

Now the renovation is complete, the two Toms are taking time to enjoy their calm, pared-back home. They've already thrown several dinner parties for friends and family, and have many more planned.

The open-plan living room and kitchen used to be two separate rooms, which the couple united to optimize the space (pages 56 and 57). The ceramic plant pots and side table were all handmade by Tom Lawson, while the lounge chair is from Made.com. Tom and Tom love to combine cooking with socializing, so they designed furniture for maximum flexibility, including the banquette and organic-shaped dining table (this page). The rice-paper pendant light is from Nordic Nest. The cupboard knobs were handmade by Tom Lawson.

A lot of the furniture and other items were created by the couple themselves because they couldn't find what they wanted on the market. The kitchen shelves, counter and even lampshade were designed and made by them (opposite). The dining table has a pine base with a hand-cut tabletop, which they finished with several layers of tractor paint to give a durable high-gloss finish (above). The chairs are Hay re-editions of Danish design classics: J77 by Folke Pålsson and J104 by Jørgen Bækmark.

61

The solid concrete kitchen counter was made bespoke for the flat, while the rest of the kitchen was built by the couple, including the shelves and asymmetric fan cover. The brown tiles, glazed with volcanic ash from Mount Etna, were designed by Formafantasma for Dzek.

The serene bedroom has a raw feel to it, with a low bed covered in layers of thick linen in natural colours (opposite). The wall-hung bedside table/nightstand comes from Toogood and on top is an arrangement of ceramic experiments by Tom Lawson. The cotton resin lamp is a prototype that was made by Tom Collison. The shelf in the bedroom is an ever-changing display of all sorts of found trinkets and handmade pieces (this page).

When the Toms moved into the apartment, they removed all the skirting boards/baseboards and coving to create a minimal space and painted the walls and ceilings with limewash. The three-legged designer chair in the bedroom is from Toogood, where Tom Lawson used to work (this page). The bathtub has been painted to match a stool from Made.com, a former workplace of Tom Collison's.

PICTURE PERFECT

British-born photographer Kate Bellm first picked up a camera at the age of 12. She has worked as a fashion photographer for a whole host of well-known magazines and high-fashion brands.

Kate grew up in London and studied in Paris before relocating to Berlin, but seven years ago she left city life behind and moved to the Balearic island of Mallorca, along with her husband Edgar Lopez Arellano and their son Sage. Edgar is a multidisciplinary artist who also happens to be a wonderful landscaper, and together he and Kate have created an extraordinary home and garden hidden away in the Tramuntana mountains between Sóller and Deià with amazing views over the sea.

When the couple first stumbled across the plot, it was home to an existing finca in poor shape, which they completely reconstructed to create their rustic mountaintop home. They designed the interiors themselves, using white tadelakt to create flowing, sinuous organic shapes that are adorned with tactile textiles and colourful collections of personal treasures. The garden

that Edgar has created is an otherworldly landscape of succulents and monumental cacti, and Kate has added touches that recall her English heritage in the form of mimosa blooms and a tumbling purple wisteria.

As a long-time city dweller, Kate says that when they first moved to Mallorca she pined for the energy and dynamism of the urban environment and found it hard to adapt to the slower, less immediate pace of island life. She missed the inspiration and cross-pollination that flows from the company of other creators, but after a while realized that all the inspiration she needed was right in front of her – mountains, wildflowers and natural beauty. This felt like something of a creative breakthrough, and Kate suddenly saw the life she was leading with new eyes. She began to document daily life in the mountains and by the sea with her camera, and these images were the starting point for her dreamy, ethereal book *La Isla*, which she describes as a love letter to Mallorca and its charms.

Currently Kate's focus is on her new venture, Hotel Corazón, which she has created in partnership with Edgar on a 16th-century estate close to Sóller. The 15 simple yet luxurious individually named rooms share earthy colours and the curving plaster details that feature in Kate and Edgar's own home, and open onto lush palm-fringed gardens, while the restaurant serves pesticide-free produce grown on site in the hotel's 50 vegetable beds.

But Kate is determined that the hotel isn't just for tourists and will also serve the local community. 'It's going to have a deli, a come-and-go vibe that's lacking on the island at the moment,' she explains. 'Rather than have to drive all the way to other villages, the "mountain people" who live close by will be able to come to us if they need bread, or a lemon or a cucumber.'

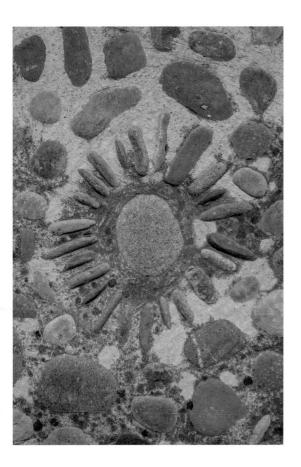

Kate's husband Edgar created lovely patterns on the paving in front of the house using stones he found around the estate (above). The charming entrance to the finca has winding stone stairs with a rustic handrail made out of old sticks and huge saguaro cacti (right). While the exterior of the property has a genuine and humble look, the inside has been totally converted into a creative, contemporary and very personal family home.

The whole front of the house is more or less covered in purple wisteria and ivy, to the couple's delight. The façade with its beautiful old wooden door has been kept untouched. The lovely handcrafted wooden sofa and table by the entrance are vintage pieces from India.

The kitchen with its fluid organic shapes was designed by the couple themselves – they achieved a smooth finish using micro cement (opposite). The white base makes for a pleasing contrast with the wooden doors, which open onto the back garden where Kate and Edgar grow their own vegetables and herbs. Taking inspiration from Indian art and design, they decorated a niche in the kitchen with tiny round pieces of mirror glass and an iron star at the top (below). The ceramic teapot was crafted by Edgar.

The living room is on its own floor a couple of steps down from the entrance and kitchen. The focal point is a huge sofa with a distinctive curved shape. A set of niches in the wall is used to display a collection of colourful decorations. The door on the far right leads out to the terrace, which offers breathtaking views over the Tramuntana mountains and the sea.

An unusual mirror hangs in Kate and Edgar's dressing room on the lowest level of the house. From the living room there is a staircase down to this floor, where Kate and Edgar have their private space: their bedroom, en-suite bathroom, dressing room and access to the garden.

OUTSIDER

NO
DANGER HERE

One step up from the entrance floor is the main bathroom (with pink walls) and after another step we find the staircase that leads up to the top floor where Kate and Edgar's son Sage has his own space. The airy white foundation and the many different floor levels make the house feel so much bigger than it actually is.

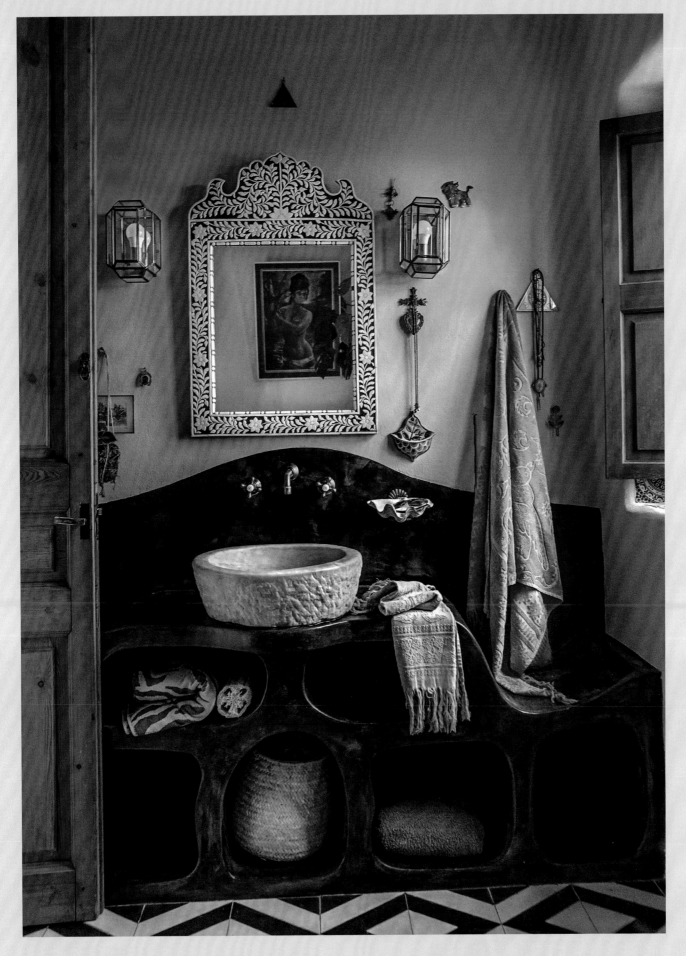

The cosy dressing room receives plenty of natural light through the windows, which also provide lovely views of the lush back garden (opposite). The main bathroom has gorgeous pink walls with taps/faucets, wall lamps and other details in gold (above).

The built-in washstand/vanity was also designed by Kate and Edgar but this time using black micro cement. By contrast, the basin is white and made out of marble. The graphic tiles are Moroccan and the white floral-patterned mirror is from India.

The pink painting in the master bedroom downstairs was made by Edgar. It's a perfect match for bedding in dusky pink, yellow and gold velvet, adding warmth and personality to the otherwise pale and neutral decor.

From the terrace, this magical sunset view over the Balearic Sea appears in the evenings, and the sunrise is just as wonderful (opposite above). It's a view that one can never get tired of. In the back garden, Kate and Edgar have a separate outbuilding where they do their laundry (opposite below). Most of the time they hang the washing outside to dry in the sun – a simple luxury. The terrace by the entrance of the house has the wisteria vine as a backdrop (above). The organic railing was made from old branches that the couple found in the garden.

83

In the summer of 2023, the couple opened the luxurious Hotel Corazón in a beautiful old house further up in the mountains (this page). Kate and Edgar stripped out the whole interior, keeping only the beautiful windows, doors and beams. The front desk was created by Yasmin Bawa, a Berlin-based artist and designer. A view from one of the suites overlooking the dramatic Mallorcan scenery (opposite).

This is one of the superior double rooms at the hotel, called the Baba Royale. The decor is reminiscent of Kate and Edgar's home, especially the modern and uniquely shaped built-in furniture covered with a tactile micro cement finish.

The largest suite, El Corazón, has a private terrace with a freestanding claw-foot bathtub, perfect for stargazing (opposite). Another guest room, known as The Sweet, has a sleek and minimal tub that blends in with the neutral walls and floor (this page).

MAKING A HOME

In 2020, chasing a long-standing dream, photographer Anna Malmberg and her family moved to the South of France, where they now live close to the wild region of the Camargue and the beautiful landscapes of Provence in a small village just 30 minutes from the Mediterranean.

The entrance of the old French house is at ground level, with a staircase leading up to the main living area (right). Cowboy boots for all sizes and genders reflect the inhabitants of this family home. A painting by Anna hangs on the wall.

Anna was born and raised in northern Sweden where she inherited her aesthetic eye from her artist parents. Her passion for photography was sparked at the age of 14, when her father built a darkroom at home. Her partner JonCha is a French writer, composer and stage director who shares Anna's passion for art and a creative way of life, a life they have spent together since they met in 2007.

After living in Stockholm, the couple moved to Paris, where Anna established herself as a photographer and their son Sonny Lou was born. After two years, the family moved back to Sweden. This was when Anna met stylist Mari Strenghielm. Driven by their shared interest in interiors and travel, they began working together and have collaborated as a team ever since. This book is just one of their many joint projects.

As well as his writing, music and theatre work, JonCha also works as a hatmaker. Inspired by road trips through the deserts of the USA and the huge agaves that grow in their village, he created his own brand, Agave Road Hats. A couple of years ago two new family members arrived: Maine Coon cats Texas and Arizona.

Anna and JonCha knew from the start that they wanted to make their 19th-century townhouse into a vibrant and creative space. Although it's rented, they have poured love and energy into creating a warm and welcoming home. The walls are painted with earthy limewash and the rooms are peppered with unique objects found at flea markets, in vintage stores or while travelling, besides many of JonCha's hats. The house has a shady terrace that's home to a well-established grapevine and functions as a second living room where the family eats most of their meals year round.

The living room could be described as the creative hub of the home, as this is where the couple works and, when they aren't working, spend time painting, drawing or making in some other way. Sonny Lou has been brought up in this imaginative environment and loves making art alongside his parents. The family's many creations are displayed throughout the home, whether they are hats, drawings, paintings or ceramics.

Anna describes her decorating philosophy as one of respect towards the architecture and history of her home and says that it's important that the environment feels cosy and inspiring as well as inviting for family and friends. She draws inspiration from the fact that she grew up in a house full of art and cites earthy tones, artists' studios, the American desert, road trips, 1970s design and music as other influences. 'I actually feel so much more inspired in my everyday life since we moved here to the South of France,' she confesses. 'I love walking around the old villages or biking with my family around where we live, and of course the Mediterranean sun is also a big source of energy, inspiration and creativity.'

A view from the hallway towards the living room and balcony doors (opposite). The rug was sourced from Copenhagen-based company Cappelen Dimyr and the furniture is all vintage. Texas the Maine Coon cat complements the earth-toned decor (this page). The eclectic artworks on the wall were all made by the family. The candleholder is vintage and the pots are from A New Tribe and Ferm Living.

The French table in the dining room is used at mealtimes and for crafting (above).
At one end is a vintage Mushroom chair designed by Maurice Burke in the 1960s.
The vase on the table was made by Sanna Holmberg. An old staircase leads up to
the bedrooms (opposite). The painting is by Anna and the stool is a vintage find.

The terrace is where the family spends most of their time (above). They love agave plants, so much so that JonCha named his company Agave Road Hats, and of course they have some on the terrace. For most of the year in this warm climate, the entry to the kitchen is screened by a curtain instead of a door (opposite).

The outdoor dining space is furnished with
rattan chairs in the style of Verner Panton
with a vintage peacock chair at the table end
(above). A vine from the neighbours' garden

provides welcome shade. A daybed on the
terrace invites relaxation (opposite). The palms,
agave and cacti need almost no attention, as
Mother Nature takes good care of them.

Anna and JonCha's son Sonny Lou loves fossils and this ammonite on the terrace was a gift to him from Anna on his birthday (above). The vintage bust comes from a local flea market.

Anna created a botanical painting for the wall inspired by the plants and the green shutters (opposite). The ceramic lion plaque above was made by her mother Kerstin.

An archway from the kitchen leads into the living room through JonCha's studio (opposite). The piano is mainly used for Sonny Lou's piano lessons. In the living room, a niche in the wall houses a lamp from Regarding Deco in Stockholm, formerly known as Swedish Nature Collaborations (above). All the walls in the house have been painted with limewash from Bauwerk in various colours. Anna and JonCha love books, both to read and as sources of inspiration for their creative work (right).

JonCha's studio is where he creates his hats and also works on his music (opposite). Artist Emilia Ilke designed the Picnic rug in collaboration with Swedish interiors brand Layered. The rice-paper ceiling light is from H&M Home. A shelving unit mounted on the wall houses JonCha's hat making tools (above). All his designs are constructed by hand the old-fashioned way. A stylish gathering of finished hats is displayed on the wall (right).

Anna puts the final touches to a painting of a dining table with chairs (opposite). Once it is complete, it hangs on the wall in the kitchen where Arizona, the second Maine Coon cat in the household, waits for dinner (above). Wooden spoons in a vintage ceramic pot, a bubbly brown candle and a vintage bowl make a charming vignette on the work surface (right).

In the main bedroom, the wall above Anna's desk is decorated with photographs, artworks and treasured keepsakes (opposite above). Anna painted the chequered terracotta pot herself and the yellow clay face and the paintings are also her handiwork. Three of JonCha's hats hang on the wall above the wardrobes/closets (opposite below). The curtain was dyed with catechu and rooibo extracts to achieve its beautiful colour. The photograph hanging on the wall by the bed was taken by Anna (this page).

The guest room is situated next to the master bedroom and has a skylight to let in the sun (opposite). The patchwork pillows come from Two Dawson and the sun sculpture is a favourite of Anna's from Austin Productions. The painting on the wall is another of her works. The third bedroom belongs to Sonny Lou (this page). Its neutral colour palette is brought to life by the mix of geometric patterns on the bed linen, pendant lampshade and rug.

URBAN OASIS

In the centre of the southern French city of Montpellier, interior designer Baptiste Bohu has created a hidden sanctuary for a client whose brief was a home suited to both relaxation and entertaining. The building was originally a large garage complete with raw concrete walls, but Baptiste immediately recognized the potential of the space and saw what he could do with the large central courtyard and soaring ceilings.

Baptiste's client Gerald asked for a home with a distinctly Balinese atmosphere, a style that Baptiste is very familiar with. They decided to plant a tropical garden in the courtyard, complete with a pool, palm trees and jungly vegetation. The interior also draws from Moroccan and Mexican interiors—other parts of the world where Baptiste finds a great deal of inspiration. The central courtyard is also somewhat reminiscent of a Moroccan riad, with its secluded feel and tranquil plunge pool.

'My aim was that you should walk through the front door, then forget where you came from. It should feel like you have gone on vacation and ended up on holiday somewhere. You should enjoy the calm of the place although you're actually in the middle of Montpellier,' explains Baptiste. 'And I think we achieved exactly this; this is such a cool and different place. Even though I've designed it for a client it has a personal feel to it, and I think this is because it is so close to my own style.'

It's important to Baptiste that furniture and lighting are authentic, so everything was chosen and sourced by him and imported from Bali and Marrakech. He even picked out decorative pieces such as baskets, terracotta jars, rugs and cushions/pillows, which were then shipped to Montpellier. As Baptiste's client is a single man, he leaned towards a more masculine style, hence the wall of glossy black zellige tiles in the dramatic bar area and the choice of clean-lined modern furniture.

Baptiste came to interior design through a circuitous route. He attended business school, where he gained his degree in finance and consulting. 'I have always been passionate about design and architecture, and for as long as I can remember I have enjoyed drawing,' he relates.

'My family was in the real estate business and my father insisted on me going to business school. This led me to studying worldwide, and my last stop was Shanghai. I started working in an advertising agency and at the same time I did interior projects as a hobby for friends. After renovating my apartment in Shanghai, it was published in *Elle Decoration* in China and in the *New York Times*, and suddenly I got many requests for residential projects. This is how it all started. If you have a passion for something, you just have to embrace it and go with the flow!'

Most of Baptiste's clients are young families and his forte is whole house renovations, including gardens, pools, interiors and furniture. Taking care of the entire design process and offering a complete solution is a creative exercise that he evidently excels at and very much enjoys. A perfectionist with an eye for detail, he chooses every single object and item along with his clients, and makes sure they are fully satisfied with the end result. For Baptiste, each and every project is a unique creative adventure and tells its own specific story.

The master bedroom on the ground floor has a unique doorway, which Baptiste imported from Marrakech (opposite). It gives the house a feeling of authenticity and is a counterpoint to the modern interior. Inside the bedroom is a luxurious bathtub with black taps/faucets from Bernstein.

Baptiste designed a sunbed for the pool area that can also be used as a bench or table (opposite). This inner courtyard is surrounded by a wall for privacy with another vintage doorway sourced in Marrakech. The living room has an amazing view of the pool that makes it hard to believe that the house is situated in the middle of the city (above).

A collection of woven rattan pendant lights hanging 5 m/16 ft up in the bar room (above). This space, which opens onto the back garden, was designed with entertaining in mind. On the wall of the main living room, Baptiste has hung a graphic monochrome rug as an unusual and tactile wall decoration (opposite). The mid-century lounge chair and matching stool were designed by Charles and Ray Eames in the 1950s – upholstered in luxurious white leather, they are both beautiful and comfortable.

Looking from the entrance through the kitchen and into the main bedroom, the iron supports of the mezzanine level give a raw, industrial feel (this page). The focal point of the open-plan kitchen is the kitchen island with its white tadelakt finish, which was also applied to the built-in shelving (opposite). Rustic bar stools carved in wood show the influence of Balinese style.

The huge pot in the courtyard comes from Morocco, just like the carved wooden door behind it (this page). In the bar area, the upholstered poufs can easily be moved around either separately or as a long modular sofa, providing maximum flexibility for entertaining (opposite). The swing chair comes from Bali and the big mirror from India. The Kilin lounge chair was designed by Sergio Rodrigues in the 1970s.

Separate from the living room and with its own entrance, the bar area was designed for parties. The wall behind the bar is covered with black handmade zellige tiles from Morocco, which is also where the custom bar stools were made. Out on the terrace, surrounded by all the jungle plants, there is an inviting sofa made of rattan for intimate conversations.

Leading up from the hallway to the loft, this staircase was designed by Baptiste. The contrast between the soft and tactile walls and the black iron is typical of his style. The statue on the right was imported by the owner.

The loft has a wooden floor, unlike the stone and tadelakt surfaces in the rest of the house (above). It is divided into an en-suite bedroom and a small lounge area furnished with an iconic LC4 chaise longue designed by Le Corbusier in 1928. The vintage Moroccan Berber pots on the open shelves are all unique and were hand-picked by Baptiste (opposite).

TELLING STORIES

A cute little townhouse in East London is home to artist Adriana Jaros and her musician partner Joseph. Both born and raised in Caracas, Venezuela, they fell in love in high school and have been together ever since.

Adriana is a multidisciplinary artist who uses ceramics, paint, paper and textiles, and describes herself as working at the intersection of art and experience. 'My purpose is to evoke emotions through rituals and processes – a cycle towards future shared and enriched experiences,' she says. Her work ranges from sculpture to murals to large-scale installations, all to the same end: 'I use my practice to retell stories – through a mural, a performance, an interior space – giving second life to a memory that has shaped me.'

A restless creative, Adriana describes herself as addicted to learning new skills and techniques. Easily bored, she is wary of becoming stuck in a rut and is constantly devising new means of self-expression. 'I am not very good with labels and find it difficult to fit into any box,' she confesses. Joseph is a musician, composer and singer. He plays the piano, guitar and synths in different bands, and is working on his own personal singer-songwriter project.

The couple has been based in London since 2011 and moved into this flat in 2020. It's a rental, but the simple interior is neutrally decorated and provides a beautiful blank canvas for Adriana's artworks. She enjoys reinventing the interior, tweaking the rooms by displaying her art in different ways. Her collages and sculptures, many of them crafted from layered paper cuttings, wood and paint, follow her home from her studio to enjoy a moment of glory adorning her home.

This studio is located on a cutting-edge industrial estate about a 20-minute walk away. Adriana describes the tiny, cluttered space as her sanctuary; a place where she stores her art materials that can be as messy as she wishes, where she can work as late as she wants and play music as loud as she likes without disturbing anyone. She finds the walk between studio and home exactly the right length – long enough to enable her to switch into work mode on the way there, and to unwind on the way home.

Adriana is currently working on a variety of projects, including a public heritage mural in her local area and a couple of mural commissions in Europe. She also has her heart set on an exhibition of her recent body of work. With her boundless creativity, talent and energy, it's evident that exciting times lie ahead.

With white walls, wooden floors and art in natural colours and materials, the staircase leading up to the home of Adriana and Joseph offers a preview of their decorating style (left). The rented townhouse flat has proven to be the perfect blank canvas for the couple's creative self-expression. Adriana in her tiny studio, surrounded by the creative chaos that she thrives upon (above).

The wooden shelving unit in the living room was designed by Adriana and handmade by Juan Junca of Studio Manolo, an Argentinian carpenter based in London (opposite). The shelf space is shared between books and Adriana's ceramic creations. She loves trying out different shapes, forms and glaze finishes from raw to glossy. The cosy and personal interior reflects the couple's professions and interests, with traces of music and art everywhere (this page). The sculpture on the side table is a collaboration between Adriana and the artist Steve Baddeley – he shaped the wood and she painted it.

The Pacha lounge chair, originally designed by Pierre Paulin in 1975, is from Gubi and so is the yellow Gräshoppa floor lamp, a 1940s design by Greta M. Grossman. Adriana and Joseph made the simple bookshelf on the floor using four bricks and a wooden plank. The iron stove keeps the space warm during winter.

The kitchen is simple but functional. Big renovations are not an option because the flat is rented, but luckily enough the space meets the couple's needs. Adriana's artwork made with recycled painted fabrics draws the eye in this calm decorating scheme. The cups on the shelf are all her handiwork, too. A wooden storage trolley from Zara Home serves as a pantry.

The living room incorporates a dining area with a vintage table that is also used for crafting. The iconic Butterfly dining chair was designed by Lucian Ercolani, the founder of Ercol, in the 1950s. Another of Adriana's textile hangings can be seen on the wall, in between a group of her acrylic paintings and an unusual piece of wood that was given to her by the artist Lee Borthwick.

Lovely morning light falls on Adriana's artworks: the wall art made with recycled fabrics, the painted wooden sculpture and the miniature ceramic pieces (this page). The bedroom walls and ceiling were painted with lime paint in a warm tone to create a calm space in which to rest and reset (opposite). Mixed-media works by Adriana hang on the wall by the fireplace and above the vintage chest of drawers/dresser.

The bathroom is quintessentially English, with an old wooden floor and a window overlooking the garden (above). Walls painted green echo the foliage outside and the brown towels are from Danish company Tekla. Even this room we find some art by Adriana – a volcanic ceramic composition with bespoke mounting and framing by Facility, a studio in London (opposite).

A DREAM COME TRUE

In the depths of the Mallorcan countryside, Swedish couple Pamela and Daniel Moell have built themselves a modern finca – a house that Pamela has been picturing for many years.

Pamela and Daniel started to search for a renovation project in 2017 and had looked at old houses in Italy and on the Spanish mainland without success when, finally, chance brought them to Mallorca. And, as luck would have it, 'We instantly fell in love!' recalls Pamela. 'We turned to a local real estate agent – who only spoke Spanish, which we don't – so when we went with him to look at a house, it turned out to be a plot of land. A plot that didn't even have planning permission, completely in the countryside. But the location was magical, so after many discussions we bought the plot and then the big job of designing the house and, above all, getting planning permission could begin.'

The couple designed the house themselves, then sought help from a local architect, who drew up the plans and paperwork necessary to obtain building permissions. 'It took us three years from first sketch to building permit, and is the most challenging thing I have done in my entire life,' Pamela declares. 'The good thing about it taking so long is that I was able to finish the interior down to the smallest detail.' The couple planned a home that was not only beautiful but would also have minimal impact on its rural surroundings. 'The house is off-grid and is completely self-sufficient in electricity (solar panels) and water (we have our own well).'

As the founder of Swedish tile company Stiltje, the surfaces in this home were a passion project for Pamela. She and Daniel visited a number of quarries on the island before finding exactly the right stone for the facade of the house. Inside, the doors are made from recycled wood, while the walls and floors are covered with an array of handmade terracotta, zellige and marble tiles, many of them custom-made especially for the house in Pamela's chosen earthy palette. These provide a harmonious backdrop for a collection of African wooden furniture, with antique printed textiles and washed linen used to cover the beds and soften hard surfaces.

Now that work on the house is finally drawing to a close, Pamela is planning to open a Stiltje boutique in Mallorca and working on a special line that's in tune with the landscape and colours of the island. 'I quickly learned that a colour that looked a particular way in Sweden looked completely different in Mallorca. Nothing could be chosen from Sweden without sending colour samples to be seen in the Mallorcan light. I got to know local craftsmen who made interior details for us locally. It felt important to be able to keep as much as possible local and get some Mallorcan soul into this newly built house.'

Pamela can trace her passion for stone all the way back to childhood, when she had a stone club with friends, collecting pebbles and rocks that they then washed, studied and put on display. The leap from hobby to profession occurred when Pamela was renovating her home in Sweden. After importing a container of tile and stone from India, she decided to sell what was left over. 'There was a lot of interest in the stone, and thus Stiltje was created,' Pamela recounts. 'Over time, I have built up a unique range of stone floors and tiles all carefully selected by me, and being able to fill this house with my products feels fantastic!'.

These beautiful ceramic pieces were made by women in Sejnane, a town and community in northern Tunisia known for its artisanal pottery (left). They were bought by Pamela specifically for the house and are seen here on the upstairs terrace. Looking down from the top of the stairs reveals part of the living room (above). The marble wall lamp was designed by Pamela and made in Italy.

This is what you call a room with a view – the truly incredible vista was the main reason why the Moells bought this piece of land. Pamela collected the furniture and decor over the years, from the Tuareg rugs and pots to the Kontiki leather sofa designed in Sweden by Arne Norell in the 1960s. It's a joy to finally see them all come together in this space.

This antique bench made by members of the Senufo tribe in West Africa was carved out of a single log (above). The wall above is decorated with vintage bamboo art from Central Africa. Pamela and Daniel's company Stiltje made the floor tiles. The upstairs lounge area has a long tadelakt bench with hemp cushions (opposite). Wooden roof beams add to the rustic feel.

The view from the far end of the house facing the terrace. To the left are two antique African birthing chairs and to the right a pair of 1950s lounge chairs designed by Ate van Apeldoorn. It took a lot of time and effort to get the perfect rounded shape and smooth tadelakt finish on the staircase.

This carved wooden object on the sofa table downstairs is a board for the game mancala made in Ivory Coast (above). The swirl of the stunning staircase ends with a built-in bench (opposite). From here there is a wonderful view of the landscape outside. Pamela has brought together vintage textiles in earthy colours with brass lamps handmade to her own design.

The main bedroom has a en-suite bathroom with tadelakt walls, marble mosaic floor tiles and a Beni Ourain rug (above). Vintage Dogon doors from Mali were repurposed for the wardrobes/closets. The floor tiles from Stiltje are called A Mano – the colours were chosen especially for this house (opposite). The vintage Lobi chair is probably from Ethiopia.

Fruit and vegetables from the garden are washed in this outdoor basin, which was carved out of one huge piece of stone (above). On the terrace, the views are framed like paintings on a wall (right). This is Pamela and Daniel's sanctuary. It is sheltered from sun, wind and rain, and because there are no neighbours for many miles, the privacy is total. The peacock chair is vintage and so are the iron chairs from Spain.

Lovely geometric tiles from Stiltje line this wall in the kitchen (opposite). The black ceramic vase is another handmade piece from Sejnane, whereas the olive branch is from closer to home – the Moells have a number of trees in their garden. As a contrast to all the white in the other rooms of the house, the couple decided to use antiqued steel for most of the kitchen surfaces (above). The Ruska tableware was designed in the 1960s by Ulla Procopé for the Finnish brand Arabia (right). Its name means 'autumn', after the warmth of the colours.

Imagine waking up to this view from the main bedroom. The headboard is an Igbo door from Nigeria and the Walanga chair was made in Ethiopia. Pamela and Daniel decided to keep the beams in the roof visible when they built the house and treated them with stain to get the right finish. The huge Moroccan rug is delightfully soft underfoot.

Kethevane's passion for creating in wood began with these carved spoons – she has carried on working with this versatile material ever since (above). All around the house we find little collections of creations in wood, paper or ceramics (opposite). These delicate pieces are sketches or prototypes of ideas that may evolve into larger works.

SHAPED BY HAND

Kethevane Cellard is a Paris-based artist. She has exhibited in France and Mexico and her work is held in private ownership in Europe and the United States, as well as in a public collection in the Paris area.

Kethevane lives and works from her family's home in Arcueil, and her work encompasses both ink drawings and sculptures in wood. Working from preparatory sketches, her drawings are of monochrome, weightless forms, while her sculptures, with their organic shapes, are defined by the play of light and shadow. Their ambiguous, hybrid forms are difficult to place in space and time.

Kethevane's house was a working sawmill until 2010, when it was renovated to create an industrial-style home, complete with brick walls, beams and skylights. The interior is arranged around a large open-plan space that was once home to the mill's heavy machinery. This area is now a creative hub, consisting of Kethevane's workshop, office, and studio, which also serves as the living room, and the stunning kitchen.

Before moving here, Kethevane was working on a series of drawings in charcoal, but one thing led to another and suddenly she found herself working with wood. 'I like to think that the house has some kind of energy that hinted me towards wood carving somehow,' she muses. 'I never decided to work in sculpture – I fell into it. And making sculpture revolutionized my imaginary world; a whole new language of forms emerged in my mind after confronting this new material. So it's a big thing. Sculpture just sort of happened to me.'

Kethevane's sidestep into sculpture happened when she fell in love with some carved wooden spoons and decided to have a go at making one herself. She bought some walnut wood and gave it a try, only to become fascinated by the carving and whittling process. She has continued carving with no specific goal in mind and while still working on her drawings. 'The confrontation with wood brought me to cast a very different gaze at the shapes I was drawing, and sculptural forms started to inform my drawings,' she explains. 'I found myself down this new path just like that.'

Her large-scale pen and ink drawings are made with a calligraphic fountain pen. The drawings are reminiscent of etchings and each one is the result of hours of

meditative work. She calls her drawings 'figures', a term used in the art world to denote the representation of a living being in its entirety.

Living and working in the old sawmill has had a positive effect on Kethevane's work, which she ascribes to the interesting history of the house and the beauty of the studio, overlooking the garden where her children play and the family's two cats sun themselves. Working from the heart of her home suits her creative process perfectly. Having previously worked as a graphic designer, she was seeking a more fulfilling mode of expression, and this mission has been accomplished.

Kethevane's desk space is colour-coordinated, neat and tidy (above). Everywhere we find scribbles and notes that document her creative experiments. The desk and drawing board are located at the back of the cosy studio, which also incorporates the family living area (opposite). This room has great daylight coming in through the skylights all year round.

One of Kethevane's wooden creations waiting to be completed (above, clockwise from above left);
by the drawing board is her favourite mug, handmade by Clair Catillaz; a sculpture made from part
of a walnut tree; a display of earth-toned pigments, bringing warmth and colour to the studio. A wall
of windows looks out to the front garden (opposite).

Huge plants thrive all year round in the sunny studio. The two art pieces on the wall to the left are Kethevane's drawings, the colourful one in the middle is by Emma Larsson and the landscape photograph on the right is by Jérôme Galland.

An iron staircase leads up to the bedrooms and other private spaces of the house (opposite). The downstairs of the house comprises an open-plan kitchen and dining area, the studio and living area, the office and Kethevane's workshop. The vintage bentwood rocking chair is a Thonet design. Light filters through the trees in the front garden, casting shadows on a collection of Kethevane's works on an aluminium stool from Ferm Living (this page).

The former owner of the house installed a restaurant kitchen in the house and used to hold cooking classes here (right). When Kethevane restored the old factory into a home, she decided to keep the old industrial features such as the brick wall and iron beams, which celebrate the heritage of the house. She further enhanced the masculine look with dark wooden floors and iron-framed windows. The dining table, surrounded by Tolix A chairs, has space to entertain many guests.

LEAP OF FAITH

For artist Sergio Fiorentino and photographer Rosita Gia, home is the former refectory of an early 18th-century Cistercian convent in the centre of the charming Sicilian city of Noto. A World Heritage Site renowned for its perfectly preserved baroque architecture, this cultured and historic city is a perfect fit for the cosmopolitan and creative couple. The former refectory is adjacent to the Church of Santa Maria dell'Arco, and its thick walls and the churchyard absorb the sounds of the city beyond. The couple say that their favourite time of day is in the early morning – they always keep their windows wide open, and in summer they can hear the swallows swooping overhead.

The couple met about four years ago, when Sergio invited Rosita to his studio to see his work. 'We love the same things – art and beauty. After living together for a while, we started working together and fantasized about publishing common projects. This dream recently came true when we published our first book, *Acqua e Oro*,' says Rosita. As well as her work as an art director and photographer, she designs clothes for her brand Archivio. Her silk and linen designs have a fluid, timeless quality, and she has just opened the Archivio Gallery and Boutique, in which she presents a curated selection of her clothes and pictures along with a variety of pieces made by other creatives.

Having previously worked as a gallerist, about 12 years ago Sergio returned to painting after a long break. He decided to leave his hometown of Catania and headed south for a fresh start in Noto, where he started looking for a new home. He was seeking a place where he could both live and work. However, nothing excited him until, thanks to a friend, he stumbled across the convent and knew he had found the right place. 'The property used to belong to the church, but in the 1800s a lot of church property was sold to private owners, and this is how I managed to get hold of it,' Sergio explains.

The building had been unsympathetically converted into an apartment, complete with false ceilings that concealed the original features and cement covering the stone floors. With the help of a friend, the Noto-based architect Massimo Carnemolla, Sergio embarked upon a complete renovation, stripping out the ugly 1970s additions to restore the original volume and tranquil beauty of the refectory. He recalls, 'I had to strip down the walls and ceiling from each of the 12 rooms in the apartment. On the right-hand side of the arch, I found traces of blue and red lime paint, and this was mind-blowing. In my paintings, these are the two colours that I use. Finding these two colours gave me confirmation that this was the right place for me to live and to create.'

The studio is not only Sergio's creative hub but also a space where he can display his art, and it has a positive, almost magical energy. In homage to the building's original function as a refectory, the couple has positioned a huge table dating from the 1960s on the spot where the monks would have sat to eat together some 300 years ago, beneath a lofty beamed wooden ceiling. Enjoying these connections with the distant past, Sergio and Rosita do not take the good fortune of living and creating in this historic space for granted.

The rather humble entrance to the former convent from the yard offers no clue of what to expect when you step inside, except for the bowl containing Sergio's blue paintbrushes (above right). Inside, the ancient and modern come together in the huge old doorways, for which Sergio commissioned industrial-style glazed doors with iron frames (right). This is the entrance to the more private part of the building, which contains an open-plan kitchen and living room and a bathroom on the ground floor, and a bedroom upstairs in the loft space that Sergio built himself.

Sergio and Rosita have decorated the spectacular living space with warmth and personality, despite its vastness (below). Plants bring life into the room and Sergio's paintings match the scale of the walls. Unusually, this is where he parks his motorbike.

Unless Sergio and Rosita have guests, they typically prefer to eat together in the kitchen (this page). The marble table is from the 1970s and so are the Lulli chairs by Italian designer Carlo Ratti. On the table is a collection of pots brought together by Sergio. A human figure and a sculpture of a dog both appear to be looking up at the window (opposite). The black dress was designed by Rosita and the book is a collaboration between her and Sergio.

Plants in silhouette against the sun (opposite, clockwise from above left); Sergio has a huge collection of Italian Moro head vases, including these yellow ones in the kitchen; a dramatic internal doorway; another Moro vase next to Sergio's brushes. He designed the gold cabinet (above, clockwise from above left); an old stone basin; textured surfaces in the kitchen.

In the couple's private space is this corner where they relax, read and socialize. Here is yet another collection of Moro heads, each with its own expression. The painting above is a portrait of Rosita. She and Sergio chose to keep the beautiful original floor tiles as a tribute to the history of the former convent.

Another of Sergio's portraits of Rosita hangs in the hallway (above). It makes for a graphic combination with the black marble table, white metal chairs from the 1960s and of course the obligatory Moro head, this one with a comic expression. Three different tiles can be seen on one small area of the floor (opposite). The painted clay fish dates from the 18th century.

The studio is not only where Sergio works, but also a showroom for his art. This space was once a refectory where the monks ate around 300 years ago. Sergio and Rosita have their own dining table on the very same spot, signifying their love and respect for the building's history. The huge table was made in the 1960s and is teamed with a set of mid-century Medea chairs designed by Vittorio Nobili for Fratelli Tagliabue.

A corner in the studio with various pieces of art created by Sergio, not only the painting and sculptures but also the iron cabinet decorated with fish (above). His furniture always has a

few secrets, and this piece is no exception – he designed it as a cabinet for ice. The back room is mainly used for storage, but it's also a most inspiring place to sit and think (opposite).

THE LOOK OF LOVE

While on maternity leave with her son Max, Lina Kjellvertz took the opportunity to visit her mother, who lives in Mallorca. One day, pushing the pram along the streets of Palma in the sunshine, Lina happened to end up looking round a shabby old carpentry workshop. The sale price was low, due to the building's poor condition and its classification as a commercial rather than residential property, but Lina could see that it had plenty of raw potential plus an ideal location, on a cobbled street right in the centre of the city. She and her husband Edin had talked for years about moving to a warmer climate when the time was right, and suddenly she felt that perhaps that time was now.

The property was undeniably shabby – the windows were falling out and the garden was an overgrown forest peppered with old junk – but Lina was beguiled by the building's beautiful, albeit neglected shell. She called her husband Edin and, despite the fact that he hadn't even seen the place, he agreed they should buy it. 'We had to sell our apartment in Stockholm and move to a smaller one. The renovation took a full seven years and cost us so many grey hairs, a number of near-divorce fights and an eternal struggle with Spanish bureaucracy,' recalls Lina. 'But now the transformation is finally done and it turned out just as I hoped it would, if not better.'

Edin and Lina founded their interior design company Dusty Deco about 12 years ago. The foundations were laid while they were living in separate cities: Edin in Paris and Lina in Barcelona. Sharing a passion for antique and vintage finds, both of them spent hours trawling flea markets near their respective homes and amassing a stockpile of 'vintage goodies'. As a result, when they both returned to Sweden and moved in together, their new home was bursting at the seams with treasures and they decided to sell some flea-market finds online. The

unexpected success of this venture took Lina and Edin by surprise, and planted a seed in their heads for a brand-new business opportunity.

Lina takes up the tale: 'One evening, we sat in a courtyard in Barcelona listening to Dusty Springfield and fantasizing about selling hand-picked vintage items to like-minded people under the name Dusty Deco. Once we got home, it turned out that these weren't just empty words. We rented a garage and quite quickly filled it up with nice objects that we collected. We started a weekend shop that became popular. We travelled quite a bit for work during that time – I worked at H&M and Edin at Acne – so we had to start off small, but eventually there was another store, and then two more, and like this it has continued. The style has developed together with us,

and nothing is allowed into the store that we can't imagine having at home ourselves.'

When the couple moved to Mallorca, they opened a showroom in Palma offering an eclectic mix of vintage pieces and artworks alongside their own range of furniture and rugs, which is produced in partnership with interior design company Nordiska Galleriet. Today, their focus is primarily on creating Dusty Deco originals, many of them inspired by iconic modern designs and vintage pieces that have passed through the couple's hands over the years.

'Right now, we are enjoying Mallorca so much,' says Lina. 'Edin gets tired of the city now and again, but then he goes on a work trip, to a market or an art exhibition, and he's happy and satisfied again.' They have many plans for the future of Dusty Deco. 'One day we dream of a Dusty Hotel in some old village somewhere, the next day it's shops all over the world and some days we just want to go back to the weekend shop in all its simplicity. In the near future, we're opening a store in Stockholm with our own brand, and we're so excited. The circus never really stands still, but that's also the fun part!'

When not in use as part of the guest suite, this lounge area downstairs becomes a second living room (above). The sofas are from IKEA with covers from Bemz, the rattan chair is from Bukowskis online auction and the travertine table is a bespoke piece from Svenskt Tenn. Vintage paintings hang on the wall.

Upstairs, the workshop space that Lina initially fell in love with has been restored and turned into a combined living room, dining room and kitchen. The original vaulted ceiling is now a lovely feature in this creative and personal home. The pendant lights over the dining table are vintage treasures from the South of France. Lina and Edin now have their own range of Dusty Deco designs, which includes the Pyramid table lamps and pink velvet-covered Lola sofa seen here.

A Howard-style armchair from Rialto Living faces a pair of Spanish chairs in wood and leather by Danish designer Børge Mogensen, originally designed for Fredericia in 1958. The shelving unit houses books and more, including Dusty Deco's Paper lamps and Swirl vase. On the wall there is a photograph of Lara Stone by Tyrone Lebon, a gift from Edin signed 'Lara to Lina, happy birthday'. It is a treasured piece that will never ever be sold.

Just a few minutes' drive from the Kjellvertz home, Lina and Edin have a showroom for their interior design business (opposite). As inspiration for their clients, they have decorated a whole apartment with furniture, lighting, fabrics and art that they love, including a graffiti-style painting by local artist Fatima de Juan. Back at home, their living room features a painting by Colombian-born artist Douglas Cantor (above). The round table is vintage and the rug is a Dusty Deco limited edition from a few years ago.

This doorway leads out from the Dusty Deco showroom to the adjoining terrace (above). A vase from Lina and Edin's Arcissimo range stands on the side table next to a Taccia table lamp – a classic modern design by Achille and Pier Giacomo Castiglioni for Flos in the 1960s. An unexpected mix of old and new is the key to an inspiring interior, according to the couple, and was the guiding idea behind this art wall (opposite). An 18th-century sofa teamed with a modern designer table completes the scheme.

Another corner of the showroom has been styled as an inspiring living room area. The distinctive Bamboo and Arco lounge chairs are Dusty Deco originals and so are the Sphere candleholders on the coffee table. To the left of the door is a large painting by Hank Grüner, who was born in Colombia and now lives and works in Stockholm. The photographic print on the right-hand side was created by Swedish artist Johan Strindberg.

In the kitchen, a window overlooks the garden and pool area and Lina and Edin enjoy the view while washing up (above). The counter is made of Binissalem stone from the island. Lighting and accessories span centuries of Swedish design, from the traditional ceramic utensil pot to the modernist wall light by Hans Bergström. The Dusty Deco showroom offers bedroom inspiration with a vintage chandelier made of Venetian glass presiding over the composition of old and new (opposite).

Siblings Lola and Max share the most creative kids' room (above and opposite). Each child has their own bed surrounded by their personal space. The lounge area in between has a lovely vintage sofa in a yellow and green floral pattern and a rattan sofa table that came from Wallapop, an online platform for buying and selling second-hand items. The art wall is a bold mix of drawings and paintings by the children themselves, together with graphic prints and vintage paintings from flea markets.

INDEX

Page numbers in *italic* refer to the illustrations

PICTURE CREDITS

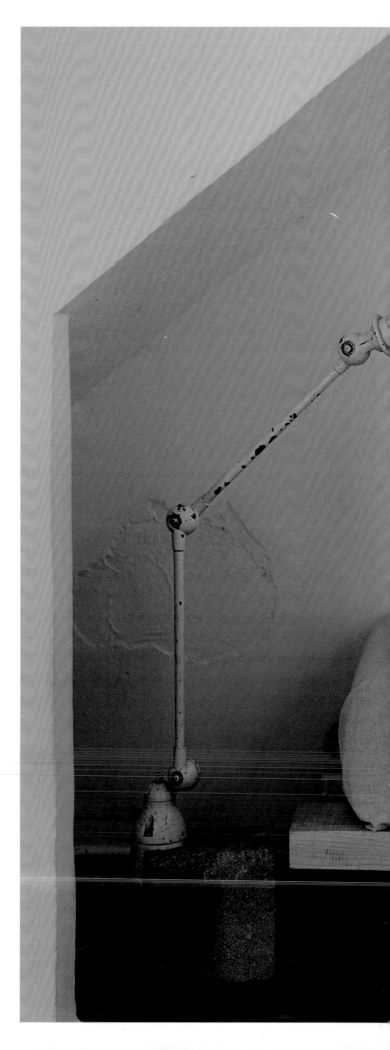

BUSINESS CREDITS

Kate Bellm and Edgar Lopez Arellano

@katebellm; katebellm.com

Hotel Corazón @hotelcorazon
hotelcorazon.com

Baptiste Bohu

@baptistebohu
baptistebohu.net
@casajunglemontpellier

Kethevane Cellard

@kethevane.cellard
kethevanecellard.works

Sergio Fiorentino and Rosita Gia

@sergiofiorentino
sergiofiorentino.it
@rosita_gia
rositagia.com

Rosita's boutique Archivio Official can be found at @archivio_official

Soraya and Michael Forsberg

@sorayaforsberg
soraya.forsberg@gmail.com

Adriana Jaros

@adrianajaros_
adrianajaros@gmail.com

Lina and Edin Kjellvertz

Lina and Edin's furniture emporium Dusty Deco can be found at @dustydeco and their flagship store is at:

Linnégatan 13
114 47 Stockholm
Sweden
dustydeco.com

Tom Lawson and Tom Collison

@tomcollison
tomcollison.com
@tomleefox

Anna Malmberg and JonCha Schwartzmann

@annamalmbergphoto
annamalmbergphoto.com

JonCha's handmade hats can be found at @agaveroadhats and agaveroadhats.com

Adriana Meunié and Jaume Roig

@adrianameunie_textilework
adrianameunie.wordpress.com
@jaumeroig_artwork
jaumeroigceramica.wordpress.com

Pamela and Daniel Moell

@pamela_moell

Pamela and Daniel's tile boutique Stiltje can be found on Instagram @stiltje.se and @stiltje.rocks and their flagship store is at:

Brahegatan 32
114 37 Stockholm
Sweden
010-516 88 93
stiltje.se

Emma Sawko

@emmasawko

Wild & The Moon @wildandthemoon

Visit wildandthemoon.com for details of restaurant locations in Paris, Amsterdam and Dubai.

ACKNOWLEDGMENTS

Creating this book together has been so inspiring and a true adventure. Yes, it was a logistical nightmare at times, but, again, the adventure!

First of all, we would like to thank the lovely and creative people that opened up their homes for us (in order of photography): Tom Lawson and Tom Collison, Adriana Jaros, Adriana Méunie and Jaume Roig, Kate Bellm, Pamela and Daniel Moell, Edin and Lina Kjellvertz, Baptiste Bohu, Emma Sawko, Kethevane Cellard, Soraya and Michael Forsberg and Sergio Fiorentino and Rosita Gia. Thank you! Without you all, there would be no book. It was such a pleasure to meet all of you – thank you for your hospitality and your time and patience when it came to answering our questions about your creative homes.

We want to thank our publisher Ryland Peters & Small for believing in our book idea and trusting us to get the job done and on time. Annabel Morgan and Leslie Harrington were fantastic to work with and always there for us, guiding us in the right direction and trying to meet all our wishes and demands.

Last but certainly not least, we would like to thank our dear families. First and foremost, a huge thank you to our partners, Christian (Mari) and JonCha (Anna). They took care of our homes and children while we spent endless days, nights and weekends devoted to this project; planning, finding homes, travelling, taking photographs and writing the text. And, of course, a special thank-you to our children, Dante and Juno (Mari) and Sonny Lou (Anna) for being such good kids – we love you so!